BIEMNOM SURVIVOR

CHOL MAKUACHLUNG

AuthorHouse™
1663 Liberty Drive
Bloomington, IN 47403
www.authorhouse.com
Phone: 1 (800) 839-8640

Published by AuthorHouse 11/28/2018

ISBN: 978-1-5462-7005-8 (sc)
ISBN: 978-1-5462-7004-1 (e)

Library of Congress Control Number: 2018914037

Print information available on the last page.

Any people depicted in stock imagery provided by Getty Images are models, and such images are being used for illustrative purposes only. Certain stock imagery © Getty Images.

This book is printed on acid-free paper.

authorHOUSE®

INTRODUCTION

At the beginning and at the end of every situation I have been through, no matter how difficult it was, and especially each time I enter a new year, I always give thanks to the Almighty Fathers who have been guiding me through the year. Sometimes I have felt it was not a good year, but when I think back day by day and how many times I have been right or wrong and how many times I have been happy or sad, I realize every year is a gift. Just as when a parent tells a child, "I have a gift for you," I'm always happy and ready to examine new packages. I always open my heart wide the first morning of the year.

I have learned that God has a solution for everything, I have learned that God sends us messages two different ways. One, there was an old lady in my village called Nyandeng Luol. A few months before the event, she made up a song in the Dinka language (Ruweng dheth ki raap Kuot ate bai aci ngaar ngap chok wen Nyanawetbil, ci mangar wei ki thon jur).The translation: *"People of Ruweng, take all your crops and belongings and leave."* Our Chief Kuot Kur stayed at home, refusing to leave from the tree in his front yard, and thus sacrificed his life to the Arabs.

The night of the attack before my brother, mother, grandmother and I went to sleep, we had an argument because my brother said, "I don't feel safe anymore. We should move tonight to uncle's."

"Do you think there is a place where life has been placed in safety?" my grandmother asked. "It doesn't matter where you go; if something going to happen, it will happen no matter wherever you are."

I'm sure there were messages from God, but there was just miscommunication on how to interpret the messages. For sure, I believe God has a reward for each of those people who were in Biemnom, South Sudan on 12/25/1983 and who went through the same situation with different outcomes. It has not been an easy thing for me to forget. For my whole entire life, since that event I been asking myself why innocent people are always victims. Up until now if there are answers, I haven't found them.

The reason I wrote this book was not only to share my family's experience that night in Biemnom on December 25, 1983, but other families' experiences as well. They were also residences of Biemnom. They experienced the same attack, and many people lost their love ones. Over the last three decades, everywhere I've gone, I've met Biemnom survivors.

In 1987, on my arrival in Khartoum, I was welcomed by Akoul Makol. She lost her husband and her brother-in-law during the attack. Even though it was in Khartoum, it felt like I was in Biemnom because she had been our neighbor just across the road, and I started thinking if what had happened didn't happen, we might not be here in this place.

In Cairo, I met with another lady whose uncle's shop was next to my father's shop. We used to play together every day. She lost her father during the attack The first thing that came to my mind when I saw her, was the picture of her during our time in Biemnom.

In 2003 in Egypt, I met my aunt, Achuiel Kur, who lost her husband, Mahol Arop, in the same attack. Achuiel Kur was the closest person to my mother. They were both from Abyei. Sometimes when my mother went to visit her relatives in Rumameer, Achmiel was the one who watched my siblings and me. The people I have been meeting over the years made me feel there was no way I could forget about this event. The best way was to speak out about it and let the world know what I've been through. That night of the attack in Biemnom many people lost their lives and their loved ones, including Kuot Kur, who was the Chief of Ruweng Biemnom.

Throughout my childhood, I never wanted to talk about how my family died, but I was constantly faced with questions. "Where is your mother?" When I answered that she passed away, some kids were polite and didn't go further, but some of them wanted to know the truth and how she died. "What happened? Was she sick?" Those types of questions kept reminding me. Those were the type of nonstop questions I've been dealing with for thirty-five years.

Today when I get together with new friends or co-workers, sometimes our conversation leads from one level to another level and I find myself in a position to answer questions about my mother and father. That made me think about writing a book about them and what happened.

More important, I thought this would be the best way to encourage young folks to value their parents. God gave them to be your parents for a reason. It is not easy to grow up without parents.

I lost my mother when I was about seven years old and the last time I saw my father, I was about ten years old. No matter how strong you are, when you lose your parents you keep feeling something is missing. It isn't wealth you need your parents to give you but rather advice.

The love that your parents give you is incomparable. After my parent's death, everybody else's parents raised me. I used to listen and open my ears really wide to the other parents when they were talking to their kids. Even now at this older age, I tell myself that some people are lucky because they still have their parents. I would be enjoying my time with parents.

About Chol and the meaning of Chol- 1

I'm Chol Makuachlung. I was born in a small village called Wundgok in South Sudan located in the west upper Nile region currently known as Ruweng state. Before the separation of South Sudan from Sudan it used to be called Upper Nile.

In Biemnom around the 1970s, there were no records or hospitals and most of my generation don't know their dates of birth. They were born at home and the only way people remembered things were through a big events - famine, for example, or if something important happened or an important person died. These were the only ways people recalled things. According to what my parents told me, I was born at home with the help of women who had experience with childbirth. A few years before I was born, there was no food and the only thing available to eat that year were pumpkins. Those who remembered estimated that was around 1975. I was born two years after that. For my parents, I was the third child in the family. The first-born was my brother and I had a sister but she passed away before I was born.

I was given a name, Chol, which in Dinka language means "replacement." This was a part of Dinka culture, When there was a death in a family, any male child born after that was named "Chol" and any female child was named "Achol." I was raised in a traditional way, which meant the child belonged to everybody, especially when it came to making a mistake. Anyone could discipline a child, not only the parents. That was the lifestyle people had living at that time.

Main sources of income- 2

The main source of income of a majority of the people was livestock. My family depended on livestock and the cultivation of crops during the rainy season, which was not year round. That meant people had to grow enough crops to last them for the rest of the year till the next rainy season came.

In the beginning of the 1980s, my family moved to a small town called Biemnom. There was an opportunity to trade there, and my father started a business. He opened a shop where he could sell and buy items. Most of the items were for domestic needs, like onions, cooking oil, slate, sugar, tea, clothes, shoes and so on.

Our lives were going well and a few years later my father began to expand his business. He opened a coffee shop and put my uncle (his younger brother) in charge to run it. At the same time, the family numbers began to increase and we became six children. Then my father decided to build another house far from the town that was located at western part of Biemnom in another area called Makuachlung, which was on my grandfather's land.

The reason he built that house was he wanted a special place for those who kept cattle to stay there keeping the cattle away from the town. That was the happiest moment for the whole family. That was the only time all my family was together. That was where I started to enjoy my childhood, but that moment didn't last long.

Family disaster- 3

Our family's disaster began in middle of 1983 during the time when the South Sudanese people started to revolt against the ruling government of Khartoum. Because of my young age, I didn't have a clue what it was about. The only thing I knew at that time was that there were people called "Anyanya." They came to Biemnom and they started collecting money in my hometown. They recruited young men and those who had military backgrounds. People who already understood the importance of the movement went without been asked.

They asked my father to join them. People didn't have a choice. Those who refused were fined or taken by force. Sometimes people were beaten for refusing to go with them. At the beginning, it was hard for the majority of people to understand what the rebellion was about. Only few people who were awarded mostly those who were educated.

I will never forget the day my father left with them. It was around evening time. I still see the picture of the whole situation when they were leaving Biemnom. I can see the sun over trees before it set, and they were facing toward the northern part of Biemnom, marching and singing a moral song about, an ex-commander called Agar Gum.

I was a little boy but at that moment I felt something wasn't right. Something was wrong about the whole situation. A few months later, everybody began to evacuate the town and move back to villages. Some people closed their shops and only a few people were left in town. The majority of the people came to town daily and spent a day in the market until evening, when they returned to their villages.

One day, rumors reached in Biemnom that the militants were on their way, coming to attack Biemnom. We escaped to one of the nearest villages called Gongkew and stayed at someone's house for a few days, someone who used to be our neighbor in Biemnom. When people said the rumors weren't true, my mother decided to take us back to the town, which was not a good choice, even though my brother and I were so happy to meet our childhood friends. I remember my brother, Dau, had an argument with my mother and grandmother about going back to the town or staying put until they figured out where to go.

They convinced Dau, telling him we were going to stay there for few days and then move to our uncle's house because he had our cows. We went back to the town.

After we returned to Biemnom, my father came home unexpectedly. He visited everyone in the family and they were surprised as it had been almost five months since he left. I remember my youngest sister was born; he had left my mother while she was pregnant. Our sister was named "Anyanya Two." My father stayed with us three days and then he left again.

<u>Confusion from the Khartoum government- 4</u>

A few months later, government forces visited Biemnom to check the situation of the people in town. I thought it was weird the way they entered the town. Before they entered, they started firing guns on the air randomly. That action scared the entire civilian population and everyone ran to find a place to hide, fearing for their lives. It was during the evening hours, and we ran inside the room.

I remember that day. My family was inside, except for my older brother and my father. They could see us and we could see them too. One of soldiers kneeled in front of our yard and started firing his gun in air. If he meant to shoot us, for sure all of us would have been dead because it was bright daylight he was looking at us and we were looking at him.

He waited there for a few minutes. We were just waiting for him to turn his gun on us. We had nowhere else to go, but suddenly he took off and ran toward the middle of the town. Shortly, they went to house of the chief of Biemnom. We didn't know what happened. Then they left the town the same evening.

The way Biemnom was built, all shops were in the middle of the town facing a big tree where people auctioned their goods. Houses were built around the shops surrounding the market. What put Biemnom at high risk was that all towns had an easy access to Biemnom. There were three main roads. One from the north, which led to Abyei, one is from the east, which led, to Mayom and to Bentiu. The third came from the west, which led to Gogrial. These were what made our town more dangerous than other small towns. When the government forces came from the north, they left facing east. Probably, they were going to Mayom or Bentiu but it was not clear as to what the purpose of their visit to Biemnom was.

That year before the Biemnom attack, many strange things happened. I remember, there was a lady related to Kuot Kur the chief of Biemnom who lived at Kuot's house but most of the time came to our house and spent whole days with us. Whenever she came, we used to gather and listen to her songs. It was amazing how many songs she knew. Sometimes we asked her if she would tell us some stories. She was one of the loveliest people, especially for kids. This had been going on for many years.

A few months before the attack, she came up with a new song that was different from the songs she used to sings for us. Even the way she was singing it was very different. I remember she used to sit outside in the shadows at Kuot's house and started singing her song. "Ruweng dhath ki raap Kuot ate bai aci ngeer ngap chok wen nyanawetbil ci mangar wei ki thon jur." ("People of Ruweng take all your crops and leave."). It wasn't until I had grown up that I understood the meaning of her song. I learned from that song that there are ways God can send a message to people, and whether they follow that message depends upon how much faith people have and how wise they are.

From my understanding, her song was a clear message that God was warning us to leave Biemnom.

I wish my mother and grandmother realized that. When the soldiers came to Biemnom, it was a signal of death for a death. Sometimes, I wish if only I had been old enough to be in charge for the family. If only I had been grown enough to tell them what to do I was scared but I was a kid and no power to make my mother and grandmother listen to me.

There were many reasons we should have left Biemnom. My uncle had come to visit us and heard what was going and asked us to move to his house to avoid the town. What the government did when they came created a big fear in people.

The government came one day and informed the local police who were acting as security for the town, not to be afraid if they heard any sounds of bullets. They assured them that soon the government was going to send military forces to protect Maluaal Bridge which was not far from Biemnom.

The morning of the attack- 5

In middle of Biemnom, there was a big tree where people gathered and sold their goods. That day, my brother and I and other children were playing under the tree. At the same time, there were people sitting under the same tree doing their own business when suddenly we saw smoke. Everybody was looking northward and we stopped playing. We saw smoke all over for a few minutes. After that, people started talking. I overheard them saying that the smoke must be coming from militants who set some villages on fire.

The militants were known for attacking people randomly, looting cows and taking young people to recruit them. I could tell everybody was scared by that smoke and the way they were talking and reacting I sensed something was not right. After we finished playing, we went home and few minutes later, my brother asked my mother and grandmother if we could move to my uncle's house, since he'd already invited us. They asked him why, and he answered that he did not feel safe to be there anymore. We had overheard people saying that the smoke might be militants attacking some villages. If that was true, it meant we were in danger because the smoke was not far from the house. The argument went on for a while and I was just listening and waiting to see how it was going to end.

My grandmother said it didn't matter where we were, that if something was going to happen, it could happen anytime. But my brother was one of those people who don't give up easily. He keeps saying the same thing over and over. Finally, trying to convince my mother, he said that since our uncle had our cows for kids to be able to have milk and a place for us to stay we should go there that night.

My mother convinced him that it was getting late. How were we going to leave the goats there by themselves? It was not a short walk to my uncle; it could take a whole day to reach there with kids. "If you really want to go," she told my brother, "wait for tomorrow morning. I will see if we can find people so we can leave as you wish and that will give as enough time to take everything with us, including the goats."

No one among us realized there was a message from God telling us to leave the town. We all failed to understand the message and it took me many years to understand how the power of God can speak to people through other people. Sometimes, people ignore it because it's not an easy thing to understand. My brother felt something bad was going to happen but my family didn't realize that. If only that night my family had the same feeling as my brother had, it would have saved the rest of my family from losing their lives.

That night my brother refused to eat because he was so upset my mother and grandmother didn't listen to him. The worst and really sad thing about that night was, it was a Christmas Eve! I remember a few days before the attack took place my mother had bought me new clothes and shoes for Christmas. I was looking forward to wearing my new clothes and shoes on Christmas morning, but it didn't work that way. I wish I could find the commander of the militant operation to ask him one simple question: Why would you attack people on Christmas day? You should have waited a day after Christmas or done it days before Christmas. This is one of the things I will never forget the rest of my life. Still, I can remember the colors of clothes and shoes my mother bought me for Christmas.

That night after we ate supper, everyone went to sleep as usual. Unfortunately, it didn't take long for them to arrive while we were all sleeping in the same room in our hut made of grass. During my sleep, I felt the room was really hot even though it was a winter time. I thought it was just me and started getting really hot. Then I opened my eyes and I saw the whole room was bright with the fire. Everybody woke up. Before we started to evacuate the room, they started shooting. I heard my mother yelling. "Why are you doing this? There are children inside!" Before she finished, she was shot. Her baby and my grandmother were shot at the same time because my grandmother was standing behind her while she was carrying the baby. All three of them fell at the same time and my brother pushed me to the corner and told me to be quiet. "They will not stop shooting if you keep making noise," he whispered, "They will know someone is still alive!" Everything just happened in an instant. The room begun to collapse and they stopped shooting, thinking everyone was dead. After they left, my brother said we should go. In no time, I was the first person to open the door. The door was made of zinc and it was so hot it was about to collapse when I tried to open. It fell on me quickly as I pushed it away with my right hand. It burned my head, arm and my right side. I went outside and I was confused which way to go because the whole town was on fire. All we saw was smoke and fire everywhere.

<u>The Last words from my mother- 6</u>

When I was outside, I suddenly saw my older brother through smoke coming out from the room followed by everyone except my grandmother, younger brother and youngest sister. Everyone started running in different directions while the place was covered with smoke. I could not clearly see them. Luckily, my older brother took me by the hand and we ran together. We hid under a bush near the house. In less than a minute, we heard the sound of a someone screaming.

"Wait here," he told me, "Don't go anywhere." He let me go and he found the screaming was my mother. She was hurting from where she had been shot. He helped her to the place where I was hiding. Then my brother told my mother and me to stay in the same place. He was going to see if he could find the rest of our people. A few minutes later, he came back with no one and said our home was completely destroyed. My brother said we have to go before they came back for us. Before we left, my mother took our hands. She said, "My children I want to tell you something. If I can't leave, I suggest it will be better for all of us to die here together, because I don't want you and your brother to suffer in this world without me."

My brother told her that we were not going to suffer as long as he was around.

Then she freed my brother's hand and said, "Dau, my son, please take care of your brother no matter what. Don't forget your brother." Then she told us to run away so we started running across the forest to the nearest village where we could be saved. I had no idea where we were going, but my brother knew the way and we reached a small village called Malual. People already knew what happened since they saw smoke all over the town. They took us to my uncle's house, the house we were supposed to go to the day before.

A few days later we received a list of bad news about my sister, cousin, grandmother, youngest sister, and my mother. They found my mother's body near to our house. They found two bodies inside the room which they confirmed were my younger sister and my grandmother. My sister and my cousin, according to my auntie, died two days after they made to her house. They died from burns while waiting for medical attention to save them. After the situation cleared in town, my uncle and other groups of people went back to Biemnom and started looking for my younger brother. They looked everywhere but there was no sign of him either dead or alive. We considered him dead. We spent a few days at my uncle's house and moved to another place called Mangar. It was where my relatives were staying and everyone started crying. The whole time, I was just running for my own life. The extent of this tragedy and the impact it would have on my life had not occurred to me. That same night, rumors reached us that militants were on their way so people begun packing and we all escaped to Mathiang Chol Ador. That place was safer because the village was on the other side of the river.

Sultan Kuot Kur, originally from the Mijuan clan, was born in a small village called Koryom, the main birthplace of Kur Kuot's family. Sultan Kuot Kur attended school during the British colonization in Sudan according to the old Sudanese school system. In the late 1960s, Sultan Kuot Kur was transferred to Mayen Abun to resume his education in intermediate school. There Sultan Kuot and his brother, Nyok Kur, were arrested and accused of being related to the rebels.

They were put in prison for investigation. During their time in prison, they planned to escape but it was not easy for both of them to do it. So, Kuot suggested he stay and his brother should leave, because if the prison guard discovered an escape, they would kill any person left. Kuot knew this and thought if they killed him, his brother at least would be alive. He knew his brother to have a revengeful heart. If they killed him, his brother would surely seek revenge. Kuot had a different heart, so he suggested that his brother leave and he would stay, pretending to be two people until his brother had gotten far enough away to no longer be sought.

After his brother escaped, Sultan Kuot was transferred to Mankien for the further investigation. After many trials and investigations, Kuot was found not guilty of any accusations. In addition, they were afraid his brother Nyok Kur might come back one day for revenge if they killed his brother. So he was released and never got the chance to go back to school.

The same year, Kuot went to Khartoum with a little bit of education. He was appointed as a member of a parliament under the President, Abrahim Abboud, and he served until the military coup by the President Gaafar Muhammed Nimeriy in 1969. Then he returned and went back to Biemnom because Nimeriy was trying to eliminate those who had served in the government of President Abrahim Abboud.

In Biemnom, he began his campaign for the Chief of the Mijuans clan. According to tradition, the chief must be from the two ruling families, Dhien Kurdit and Paowjiek. Kuot Kur was from Dhien Kurdit and on the other side, his brother Nyok Kur Kuot was running against him and supported by Ruweng, while Kuot was supported by his relatives. Relatives had more power than clans and they had a right to choose who they think is the best choice to rule the people.

Therefore, Kuot Kur was able to win against his brother and succeed Awojak Chol Kuot. People had not been happy with Awojak. He succeeded his father, Chol Kuot, and during his rule, many people suffered a lot from too much enforcement of the rules. All Ruweng Biemnom clans were complaining about him when his son Awojak Chol became the sultan of Ruweng Biemnom. People thought maybe he would do as his father had done.

Sultan Kuot Kur became the best choice for the people of Ruweng Biemnom. He was the paramount chief of all Ruweng Biemnom clans, according to their arrangement, followed by the deputy and the rest of chiefs:

1. Sultan Kuot Kur Kuot representing Mijuan and paramount chief of all Ruweng Biemnom clans.
2. Meyom Ayii representing Amaal clan
3. Mayik kiir Deng representing Mantieng clan
4. Yaw Kur Mabil representing Thiyeir clan
5. Thon Adul representing Abang
6. Mayik Ajarak Malith representing Nyongchiel.

On top of that, Sultan Kuot Kur was the paramount Nazather and the head leader of all chiefs according to clan's size and a civil administrative arrangement that had been going on since the British colonial rules established many years before. Ruweng Biemnom contained six clans and they were part of twenty- seven of the Ruweng clans. Ruweng itself was divided into three groups

1. Panaru
2. Paweng
3. Ruweng Biemnom (Alor Kur Kuot)

Ruweng Biemnom clans are originally from Dinka Pandang located at the Upper Nile region, where the main spoken language was Dinka and they shared the same culture and traditions as the other the Dinka groups. Their main sources of income were cultivation and livestock. Before the events and disasters in Biemnom, Sultan Kuot Kur's family was large with two houses, one at Wundamadh and the main house in Biemnom town where he spent most of his time solving civil cases. Sultan Kuot Kur was married to seven wives:

1. Ateda Koshkon Dau
2. Abuk Mejak Dau Bul
3. Nyanlang Thon Deng yout
4. Nyawei Rador
5. Nyadat Tong
6. Akar Akoi
7. Nyantung Nyok

The end of the Sultan Kuot Kur's rule- 8

Sultan Kuot Kur Kuot ruled the Ruweng Biemnom clans from the early seventies till December of 1983, when he was killed by the militants according to the eyes witnesses, first responders and survivors from the Biemnom attack. After few months, when the Khartoum government withdrew their forces from the town of Biemnom, Sultan Kuot received a letter giving him a choice of three districts he could move to - either Bentiu, Abyei or Gogrial. Kuot refused, believing it would be shameful for the chief to go to another place and leave his people behind. His answer to the letter was if Ruweng had to be killed, he would be the first person to die in front of his people.

That's what happened exactly early in the morning of December 25th, of 1983. When the militants attacked Biemnom, the first place they targeted was Sultan Kuot's house followed by the closest neighbors. According to eyes witnesses, they called him to come out, so he put on his dress including the flag. Then he came out and sat on his chair, where he was shot in the head. Inside Kuot's compound, there was a man in one of the rooms named Majok Loy Kuot, Kuot's cousin. A police officer serving the government, he was just visiting Biemnon on vacation. He saw what happened to Kuot and he came out with his gun and started fighting back but, because of militants' large number, he was shot and then ran away for his life.

After that, militants begun firing guns randomly everywhere and set houses on fire. They killed many people including Kuot's uncle, Mahol Arop and Kiir Bollath who was Kuot's police guard. After the militants left the town and everything was cleared, people began gathering and the Mijuan clan came and took Sultan's body to Pangok Abang for the burial.

One of the Biemnom survivors- 9

Achuiel Kur Shean was originally from the Abyei region, born in year 1955 in a small village called Rumyom. She was married to Mahol Arop Chom who was from Twic Gogrial. Late in the 1970s, she and her husband moved to Biemnom for her husband to practice business in Biemnom.

Her memories: *All my children were born in Biemnom. Everything went well for a while till the end of 1983 when Biemnom was attacked by the militants under the government forces.*

Early in the morning, I heard gun shots. My husband said, "Maybe these are forces who are supposed to come from Bentiu to protect civilians because of the ongoing situation." But the gun shots never stopped and began to increase more and more. Then I began to hear people talking, asking Kuot to come out. We used to live at the same compound so it was easy to hear people from the other end. I could hear Kuot Kur saying, "I'm putting my clothes and flag on," and gun sounds were still going on. When my husband opened the door, he saw Kuot on the ground. I remember he said to me, "They killed my nephew, Kuot."

Then he jumped out of the room. I tried to pull him back, grabbing his clothes to stop him from going there while I was carrying a baby on my arm. I couldn't stop him. Right in front of the porch he was shot and they set the room on fire. I closed the door and told my children to keep quiet. We hide under beds at the same time I was slightly hit by a bullet on my leg. I'm sure it was the same bullet that shot my son, Arop, on his foot. I waited until everything was clear so I opened the door and saw my husband and Kout on the ground. Then I saw Yom Malual came from Mayom with goods. He was supposed to leave in the morning. I saw him coming out of smoke, and I remembered he was sleeping inside my husband's shop. He crawled on his knees and then he ran toward the river. I believe he was the one who went and informed Mahol's relatives about the events.

Before we left the house, Nyannak and Nyankoor came. They were in bad condition as their bodies were all burnt by fire. So, I asked my daughter, Aluel Mahol, to help me with the baby then I took my wounded son, Arop Mahol, and walked toward Agonbek. We hid at the bushes for few hours and heard people's voices. We came out and followed where the sounds of people came. We met people who came from the burial of Kuot Kur. Also I meet Makuachlung, father of Nyannak and Nyankoor. I also met a person related to my husband who had been looking for me and the kids. He took the kids and me across the river where Mahol's burial was taking place.

The next day my brothers Kiir and Shean came and took me to their house at Rumyom. One day, my brother went to the Rumameer Market where he met Aguek Kon Yak. He informed him about the news of my cousin Nyanjur who was killed and the rest of the children. The only children left were Dau and Chol, so I went to Rumameer and never saw them again till I met Chol in Egypt of 2003. I met Dau in 2006 in North Carolina.

Mathew Wethait Poik from the Abang clan was one of the first people who responded to the events of the Biemnom attack. He was born in 1953 in Biemnom, joined the rebellion in 1970 till the Addis Ababa agreement in 1972 between rebels and the Khartoum government under the President Gaafer Muhammed Nimeiry. After rebel forces were dissolved into the government forces, he was stationed in Wau, which was located in the Bahr El Ghazal region till he was transferred in 1974 to Aweil in northern Bahr El Ghazal. Early in the year 1983, he was transferred again to Western Sudan and was stationed at Al fashir while his family remained at the upper Nile region. He recalls:

On December of 1983, I requested permission to visit my family who lived in one of the Biemnom suburbs known as Gongkew. To get there, I had to go through many connections from El fashir to Abyei, Ramameer to Biemnom. When I arrived in Abyei, I went to Bol Kiir's house. He used to live in Biemnom, and had been shot by unknown people. It was one of the reasons he moved to Abyei, because of security reasons.

During my stay with Bol Kiir, I met one of the soldiers I had known for long time. I cannot remember his name. He just returned from Biemnom. He was a commoner who let soldiers visit Biemnom. He explained to me the situation about security and that they had seen suspicious people. He assumed them to be rebels because they had guns when their forces approached the town.

"They ran away," he said. "We challenged the town by shooting our guns, but they did not fight back or anything. We thought they would respond. They didn't, as if we were a friend. If I were you, I wouldn't go there," he told me. The next day, two guys, Musa and Al tahar, who used to own shops in Biemnom invited me for dinner. At the dinner table, they told me the reason for the dinner was to give me some advice since I was going to Biemnom.

"Biemnom is now in a very dangerous situation.," they said. "Go and tell Kuot Kur to leave the town as soon as possible, either to come here or to go Bentiu till everything gets back to normal. His stay encourages residents not to leave the town. Also, we heard that there are rebels who stay in the market during the day. If this is true, it may cause a problem one day to residents and to him. In addition to that, tell Monyluak Majak he needs to leave too.

"Last time when he was accompanied by soldiers, they came back with news and they found suspicious individuals who appeared to be rebels. Biemnom is not a safe place for running a business anymore.{"

On the 12/14/1983, on my way, I had to stop at Rumameer to catch a Lorry to Biemnom. I met another person from Nuer who used to be in service in Biemnom and had deployed to Rumameer. He also advised me not to go there, telling me that if rebels find out I worked for the government, they would kill me. I convinced him that I was not going inside the town. My family lived at one of the Biemnom suburbs. I waited all day but no Lorry came to go to Biemnom till evening. When the temperature dropped, I started walking all night and reached home around two or three in the morning. In the evening, I went to Kuot Kur's house, the chief of Biemnom, to tell him exactly what Musa and Al tahar told me. I suggested they leave and go somewhere else or to Bentiu. I asked them if they could send more forces to protect residents, but he rejected my suggestion. He told me he was not going anywhere, since this was where he came from. This was what we called Alor Kur Kuot. He said we needed to stop being soft and then turned away from me and begin signing. I didn't get chance to meet Monyluak Majak to tell him the warning. At the same time, I felt he might reject it as Kuot had so, I went back to my house at Gongkew.

Early on the morning of December 25, 1983, my brother,Wor Poik, came to where I was sleeping and told me he heard gun sounds coming from the direction of Biemnom. It came to my mind that something bad must be happening in Biemnom. I put on my clothes and asked him to stay with our family. I ran toward Biemnom and before I even went far, I saw smoke all over the place. On my way before I reached the town, I met two children (boys) and asked them who were their parents? They answered they were Kuot Kur's children. I told them to keep running and follow the same road till they found houses. In a short distance after that, I met a man who was escaping from Biemnom. His name was Mathok Magueth. He asked me where I was going.

"To Biemnom to see what is happening," I told him.

He said nobody was there. Everyone run away and some people had been killed.

"Let us go and see if there are people who are still alive and may need help."

When we arrived, we met Chan Thon who was a guard for the chief, Kuot Kur. He was wandering and didn't know what to do.

"We saw Kuot Kur's body lying in front of his house according to the eye witness," he said. "They said militants asked him to come out of his company and shot him outside."

"Did anyone run after them?" I asked Chan Thon.

"No, we didn't have enough forces to fight with them and it seemed to be a large number of people. Didn't even try to follow them."

I believed they were not far from the town, since we could still see smoke and fire flames. On their way, they stopped at Wundgok and set houses on fire but no one was hurt. Their residents ran away to hide from gun sounds when Biemnom was attacked. As we were speaking, I saw a group of people coming and they went straight to Kuot Kur's house and took his body to Pangok Abang for the burial. I'm sure those people were from Mijuan clan. I asked Mathok to help me collect the rest of the dead bodies on the ground. We put them inside the rooms, gathered tools and enough people to help us for burial, and we headed to Monyluak Majak's house. We found his dead body along with his brother, Meyom. His body was lying in front of his shop while Monyluak's son around the age of two and half years was sitting beside him. That was one of the saddest things I have ever seen.

Before we collected Monyluak's body, a lady came and asked if she could take the kid. She took the kid and we put Monyluak and his brother Meyom's body inside a room. Then we moved to the other side of the town. We found two bodies, which appeared to be Mayen and Angoi. These were guys are from Twic Gogrial who owned shops in Biemnom. They were there for many years so we put them inside too. We went Mahol Arop's house and saw a large number of people who came on the other side of river who seemed to be his relatives. They collected his body and took it across the river for a burial to avoid further attack from the militants in case if they decided to come back.

The number of people in our group became larger. The next thing we did was to check house by house that had been destroyed by fire completely. Inside Kuot Kur's house, we found Kiir Bollath, one of his guards, burnt inside the room. At Makuacklung's house, we found two bodies. One was an adult and the other was a child. According to their relatives, the adult was Nyanajeth Pingamiit, the baby was Makuacklung's child, and the last body we found was Nyanjur Ajing, identified by his relatives.

After that, we went under a tree to rest because the sun became really hot and people became tired too. We gather all the dead bodies found and counted ten plus two children who died the following day from fire. Those made a total of twelve. Three children, two women and seven men. According to the relatives and family who knew them, they were the following:

1. the Sultan Kuot Kur Kuot
2. Monyluak Majak Machar

3. *Meyom Majak Machar*
4. *Mahol Arop Chom*
5. *Kiir Bollath Jang*
6. *Nyanjur Ajing Yak*
7. *Nyanjeth Pingamiit*
8. *Nyannak Makuacklung*
9. *Anyanya-two Makuacklung*
10. *Nyankoor Arwal Majak*
11. *Mayen*
12. *Angoi*

Mayen and Angoi were just known by their first names. As I mentioned previously, they were from twic Gogrial and moved to Biemnom to run their businesses. After we finished the burials, everybody left the town to avoid another attack. Four days later, I moved my family to a safer place then I left for El fashir to continue my duty.

Appreciation of my brother- 11

After few days, the wound on my arm started getting worse and more painful, especially at night. Sometimes, it got stuck to the mattress. I couldn't sleep because of the flies, and the only way I was able to sleep was when my brother watched over me for the rest of the night with a feather chasing the flies away. The same thing happened during daytime. He sat beside me with feather and chased the flies away so I could get some sleep. He kept doing that for some days till I recovered a little bit. I began to realize my life was really in danger. I didn't even know if it was day or nighttime. One day, I overheard my uncle's wife and other women talking about my situation. They said, since I made it this far, nothing would happen to me for sure.

In the next few days, I started to feel better so one day, I asked my brother, can you go get me a fish?"

"Let me see if I can find a hook," he said.

Luckily, he found one but the deal was, the first two caught had to be given to the owner of the hook. He was very eager, quick and was so happy when I asked him for a fish. I didn't know what was going on, but I learned later the reason. The whole time I have been there, I never wanted anything to eat. To him, my asking for something to eat was a good sign, a sign I was beginning to live again. According to him, he waited till I fell asleep before he left for fishing. He took my cousin's bed sheet to cover me from flies.

During my sleep, a cow came from nowhere and grabbed the sheet that I was covered with, but there were people sitting under a tree near where I was sleeping who saw what was going on so they rushed towards me and chased the cow away. Their intention was to save me from the cow stepping on me. At the same time they were able to save the sheet. I wasn't aware what happened since I was still sleeping. When I woke up, I found myself in middle of people.

"Where is your brother?" was the first thing they asked me.

"He went for fishing. He may still be there," I told them.

They took me and asked me to stay with them until my brother came back. A few hours later, Dau arrived with fish. I was so ready to eat that I felt I couldn't wait for them to be cooked.

I'm not really sure how many days passed before, my father came to us and brought some medicines for me because he was told about my situation. He spent some days with us and gave me a little more. I felt stronger after my father came and his presence gave my brother a break. But I can tell he wasn't happy at all.

"I will do my best to keep you safe and I'm going to find a way to take you to your uncle's house," That was the only thing he said.

Uncle's house -12

Probably a month later, my uncle (on the maternal side) came and asked my uncle (who was my father's cousin) if he could take us with him. We went to his house at Rumameer and there we were greatly welcomed because my uncle had a good relationship with my father. They were really close to each other. They grew up together at the same place, at the same time. My uncle's wife was my father's cousin. We felt she was like an auntie.

When we arrived at my uncle's house, It was my first time I once again felt at home. It was amazing the way we were welcomed to the family.

"Your father and his brother were raised by my mother after their mother passed away; there is no reason for me not to take care of you. This is your home. Welcome to the family. You are not going to sleep hungry and whatever my children eat, you will have the same." That was the first thing my auntie told us.

For the first few days, I stayed inside the house trying to learn the environment. One day my uncle's kids encouraged me to go outside to play. My uncle's house was located right on the main road where people used to go and get water including the soldiers who were serving in that area. We went outside and I started playing with my cousins and some other kids. For a few moments, I wasn't paying attention and then suddenly I saw a truck loaded with soldiers passing us. They had weapons and, they shouted and that scared me to death. I ran back to the house straight into the room where my grandmother Ayakdit was and sat beside her. "Who is this?" she asked.

"This is me Chol," I said to her.

"Are you okay?" she kept asking me.

"Yes, I'm okay."

Just few minutes later, my playmates followed me to the room making fun of me, mocking how scared I had been of the military. From what they were saying, my grandmother understood what was going on. She got mad and chased them away.

"What is wrong with you kids? You don't have mercy. This child is heartbroken," Grandmother said. Maybe the military reminded him about what happened to his family in Biemnom. Could you please just leave him alone?" Grandmother asked and then they left.

She turned to me. "You are safe from those soldiers. We are here to protect you. I completely understand where you are coming from, but hopefully you will get used to this type of situation." Grandmother said.

My wounded arm begun to heal as my uncle was a medical doctor and provided me with enough medicines. Everything went well.

One day, my brother went to Rumameer Market and recognized one of the soldiers who used to be in Biemnom. A long time before he was deployed to Rumameer, that person knew all my family. He was a good friend to my brother. My brother told him what happened to our family and he was really sorry about the situation. Every day, he brought a lot of food and stuff for me and my brother. At the beginning, I used to refuse it. "How can we eat food from people who killed our family?" I asked my brother.

"Arabs are not all the same; some of them are good," my brother told me.. "What happened to us in Biemnom has nothing to do with him. He seemed like a nice person." He was correct. He became a very close friend to my brother and everything went well for a while until my uncle decided to send my brother and his older daughter to Abyei for school. At that time, all schools, as well as the hospitals, were closed in Rumameer and transferred to Abyei. That decision wasn't good for me.

After my brother left for school, my world turned upside down. It was a tough situation for me. Everything changed and felt different. I don't know why but, something was wrong. I started to feel alone, even though my uncle had kids about my age.

I thought it was going to be only two or three months but one day, I asked my auntie how long my brother would be gone. She said he would be gone for eight months and that was really bad news for me. It meant there was no way to get out of this. One day, as I was sitting under a tree next to my uncle's house out of nowhere, I came up with a crazy idea. The next morning, I pretended

I was sick because I knew there was no hospital and the only place I could go was Abyei. My trick worked.

"Since you are sick, I'm going to talk to one of the lorry drivers to see if he can take you to Abyei," My auntie told me.

Luckily, the driver agreed and she sent me with her daughter, Achai. She was a little older than I was and she was more familiar in the place. So we took a lorry in the morning and rode all day. We arrived in the evening and went to Kuol Kon's house to meet my brother and my cousin. I was excited to meet my brother unexpectedly. We spent few hours and left to one of my mother's relative's house. His name was Aduk Deng and he provided us with a place to stay as long as we liked. His house was not far from where my brother stayed so it was easy for him to come every day.

After school, he spent some time with me, and that went on for a while. Then one day, my cousin took me to stay with my brother for a little while. After we spent time with him and my other cousin, she said we had to return before the sun set. On our way, back I saw something was blowing in the wind. It was coming our direction. Then I realized that it was a money - ten Sudanese pounds. I picked it up very quickly without wasting time and put it in my pocket. While I had the money in my pocket, I started thinking what to do with it because I was sure if I gave this money to my uncle, my brother was going to get nothing from it. My uncle was very strict when it came to money. His mindset was, money is a very easy way for children to get lost in a city and that's why he wanted none of his children under his care to know anything about money.

I thought of keeping it and giving it to my brother the next day. My cousin had already seen it, so there was no choice. I had to give it to my uncle. a few minutes later, she began asking me how much it was.

"I don't know but it looks green." I came up with a random color to avoid too many questions. We kept walking and when I reached the house, I turned around and started running away from her. I decided to go back to my brother.

"Where are you running? Come here!" she exclaimed.

"I'm going back to my brother," I told her.

When I entered the house, they thought something had happened to us, or someone was chasing me. I went straight to my brother and asked him to come with me.

"I wanted to show you something," I said and gave the money to him.

"Where did you get this?" he asked.

"From the street; it was blown by the wind," I told him.

"Did anyone seen you?" he asked me again.

"Nobody, the only person was my cousin but I ran away from her to give it to you. Now it's your choice to keep it or give it to uncle." I said.

"Did she know how much you found?"

"No. The only thing I told her was it looked green," I answered him.

"We have to take this money to our uncle. I don't want him to be mad at us, but before we go, I have to do something, since she doesn't know how much it was just that it's green in color," my brother said.

"How many Sudanese currency with green colors"? I asked him.

We exchanged it for two fives. I gave him five, and kept the other five. I needed many things for myself.

He did exactly what he wanted and he took me to the house where my uncle was. I had been worried there would be a problem because I'd gone back to my brother before I came to him. I thought bringing back the money with my brother shut down all questions.

Before we returned to Rumameer, we received a message that everyone in that particular place had to evacuate the town for security reasons. My uncle went to Rumameer for an emergency visit. After few days he came back with all his family to Abyei.

First time to attend school- 13

Abyei was my first place to attend school. After everybody left Rumameer to Abyei, my uncle found a house and we all moved in to that, including my brother. We became one big family. My uncle had two wives, so there were a good number of children but, everything was under control. He was able to feed everyone especially those who attended school. There were five of us who went to school and he provided us with school informs and all school needs. It was amazing. During the rest of 1984, everything went well, until school closed. We were getting ready for the school new year. There were almost three months left before school would open again. There was nothing to do, just playing, enjoying our holiday time. Sometimes, my aunt sent my brother, my cousin and me to the Abyei Market to buy her tea and sugar. During the market days, which were Thursday and Friday, she sent only my brother because those were busy days and many people came from villages to buy enough items to last them for the whole week.

One day my brother went to buy tea and sugar for my aunt as usual. At the market, he met with people from Biemnom and they knew us too. They started to talk and exchanged questions. Those people told him that they had left our father the day before. By that time we had gone almost two years without hearing from him. My brother didn't have a second thought. At the end of the market, when everybody started to leave, he asked them if he could go with them. Somehow, they agreed, but before they left, he did a very smart thing. He went to one of my uncle's friends who owned a shop and told him to tell my uncle that he's going to a village with these people. They are taking him to my father because they knew where he was. At the house, my auntie started to feel uncomfortable. She was worried about what happened to Dau. We were waiting all evening until nighttime but he didn't return home. When my uncle came home, he told us that my brother left for a village with some people to meet with our father. Those people had just come back from Bilpam.

In 1985, several youths from Abyei joined the movement, as one of them recalls:

My name is Aguek Kon Yak from Abyei. I was born in 1950. My education level, according to Sudan's old school system ranged from basic to intermediate. I finished school in 1968, and then started working at Abyei's hospital as a nurse. After that, I joined some medical assistant training at El obeid till I became qualified as a doctor. I was transferred to Rumameer's hospital in 1976 till 1980. I was transferred back to Abyei's hospital till I joined the movement on 02/15/1985.

Early in 1985, a group of the Ngok youths who were in Abyei decided to join the movement. We came up with a plan to find a safe place where we could do our secret meetings and other activities, a place no one could find or know about. We choose a day and time of a week for meeting, which is the best for us to meet. We asked Dr. Frances Ayom to use his clinic as an office for meetings. We chose Tobey Aduk Deng as the chairman of the group and then we started the recruitment. We were able to collect a good number of people. These were the people who joined the movement:

1.   Dr. Aguek Kon Yak
2.   Dr. Frances Ayom
3.   Tobey Aduk Deng
4.   Deng Aguer
5.   Dhaar Dut
6.   Majak Bol Atem
7.   William Bol Pallak
8.   Mading Jakang
9.   Mayen Chenyeuth
10. Lual Kachwaja Chol
11. Kuithzie Dengchol
12. Deng Amachkuoj
13. Adop Deng
14. Akoi Nyael
15. Wol Chol
16. Nyang Deng
17. Deng monytoj
18. Awan Abyei
19. Alor Bullabak
20. Ajing Anyang Alor
21. Bullabak kon

There were more people but I can't remember their names, not to mention children who were grown enough to join the movement. We came to an agreement and this had to be approved as soon as possible before some of us lost morale. We had to choose a location for us and for our families for all of our safety. We agreed to meet on Thursday on 02/15/1985.

Thursday was the best because it was the only day of the week people came from villages to Abyei's market to buy goods and auction theirs. Some people even came to sell cows and goats. The next step was any of our members who have family have to notify his family and explain the situation and advice their wives about how dangerous it would be if the government realized what we were doing. During our meeting, we chose one location called Mayen Abon as our meeting point. In addition to that we had to mixed ourselves in with those people who came from villages, so we could leave at one time using the Thursday crowds of families who live outside town as camouflage.

Therefore, I left around 5:00 pm, which was the most crowded time with people who were returning their homes. I went straight to Mayen Abun, which was the meeting point for us for gathering ourselves. Then we went to Mathiang, which was the headquarter for the SPLA. There we were highly welcomed by the chief commander Malou Kuol. The next day, we were distributed to different divisions according to our experience and military backgrounds. I was put in medical division where I served as a doctor in the surgery division. In the summer of the same year, I received bad news about Tobey Aduk Deng, Deng Aguer and Deng Amachkuoj who were members of the group who joined SPLA at the same day. Chief Commander Malou Kuol and his brother Mabek Kuol was killed by the government forces. Tobey Aduk Deng was an active police officer in Abyei and already had a military background when he joined the movement. He was greatly welcomed by the SPLA that qualified him to be in front line.

Some of our members returned and surrendered themselves to the government because of the hard life in the movement. Some lost their lives and those who survived during the struggles had reached a high rank in the military while some had retired due to their ages. I continued my service till 1989 when I was assigned to the one of the clinics at a small area called Akon to treat people who had been injured in different battlefield. After a long service, I retired from the SPLA duty in 2006. Then I moved to one of the villages called Anet and opened my own clinic to continue services and help people in that area.

Our escape from Abyei- 15

A few months later in the winter of 1985, after my brother left for the village in search of my father, all families had to leave Abyei. We left in the evening at the end of market when there was a big crowd of people so the government couldn't identify the local residents of Abyei who were moving out from those who came to the market from distant villages. We have no idea where we were going. We went to a place called Gagyum. We settled at one of our relative's houses for a few days. I didn't know what the plan was, just followed what my auntie told me, hoping everything would be okay.

One day, some kids and I were taking goats to the grassing field. On our way, I kicked something and thought it was just a stone. It rolled to the front of one kid, named Morris Aduk Deng. When he saw it, he ran towards me and pushed me away. I was shocked. He was a little bit older than I.

"Do you know what you just kicked?" he asked me. "That thing is a weapon and it can kill all of us and everyone else!"

We waited for few minutes but nothing happened. Then he took it and put it in a hole under a tree. He covered it with a grass so no one could see it and we took our goats to the grass field. The plan was, when we returned home in the evening, sometime before the sun set, Morris would come to the house where I stayed with someone named Kuol Deng Laam. He was one of the leaders of Anyanya-one, the group continuing the Anyanya movement of the First Sudanese Civil War that ended in 1972. He started asking me some questions. He asked me how I discovered the weapon. I told him I didn't know what it was. I was just walking on the roadside trying to control goats from running away from me.

Later, my uncle came home and we were all happy to see him because we hadn't seen him since we left Abyei. According to him, they went first to report themselves to SPLA camp, and he came for a short visit to his family. The next day before I took goats to a grass field, I suddenly I overheard him and the person whom we stayed was talking how they were welcomed. I felt this must be interesting so I acted like I was untying the goats, but I was listening to them. He asked my uncle

"What rank did they give you?"

"I don't know yet but I'm hoping it's something good," my uncle replied.

"You shouldn't have any problem because your brother-in-law is a sergeant major. Did you meet him yet?" the man asked my uncle.

"Yes. He wanted me to bring his son but, I don't want to right now because I need him to help the girls take care of the goats."

Then I went with some other kids who were familiar with the area to the grass field. It wasn't an easy job. We had to sit under a tree and watch them. We had to arrange who will go first, when the goats run away. Our job was to keep them in that particular area for a whole day until evening. When I came home, I went straight to my aunt and told her exactly my uncle's plan trying to keep me to watch goats.

"I'm not going to let this happen," she said. "If your father wanted you to come there, then that means that you have to go. We will find someone else to help us."A few days later, my aunt told me I was not going to take goats for grassing because I was leaving with my uncle. That was a great news for me and I was so excited, I couldn't wait to leave that day.

We left the house and it took us about a day and half walking but I was happy to meet my father and brother. I didn't even care how far it was. The bad thing was, I thought we were going straight to my father. I didn't knew he was taking me to my other uncle (my father's brother) at a cattle camp. When we arrived in the morning, everybody was busy doing something. Some of them were getting ready to take cows to the grass field and some of them were milking cows. Before we entered to the cattle camp, my uncle pointed a person from far away and asked if I recognized that person.

"Not really," I said. "That's not my father."

"I know that is not your father," he said.

After we came closer, I recognized him. It was my uncle Kiir Majak. That made me mad. "I hope I'm not here to stay at the cattle camp with him," I said.

"You have no choice," he answered.

My Uncle Kiir told me I had to stay with him there for a few days. My father was not close by and he had to find someone to take care of the cows before we left because it was going to take us maybe two or three days of walking before we reached my father's place. So I spent a few days with my Uncle Kiir, but I was uncomfortable. I had never been at a cattle camp before, I had no idea what it was like. I was wondering the whole day where I was going to sleep that night because I didn't see any room. I spent my first day with the old people whose job was to make ropes and woods that were used to tie the cows after they come back from grass field. Each cow had to be tied on its own ropes and wood to stop them from moving around or fighting each other. Also, this was the best thing to prevent calves from sucking milk from their mothers. The whole day went very slowly and I wanted it to go fast so I could see how is the night was going to look like. But even before it was dark, all the boys about my age returned with calves to the cattle's camp and tied them around the fire place that was made of dry cow dung. Then they started collecting dry cow dung to make more fire. The main reason for the fire was to make too much smoke to chase flies and some insects away because they were a threat for cattle. A few moments later, all cows were tied and the ladies started to milk the cows. I was just stuck with those old guys. After the ladies finished milking the cows, I was given milk. I thought maybe food would follow, so I waited, but it was time to go to sleep. I was given a mat made of cow's skin and spent a very uncomfortable night. I was the first one to wake up in the morning, ready to leave.

The only thing that was on my mind was to go to meet my father and my brother. A few days later we left the cattle's camp. On our way before we arrived, my uncle told me I was not going to meet my father, only my brother. My father had just gotten married and he might not be there because he was in the process of collecting cows for the marriage. I was going to stay with my brother and stepmother. He was right. After we arrived at SPLA camp, we were directed to the head quarters because my father was in the headquarters division. I met my brother and it was a great happiness. I was so ready to see my stepmother. I thought she was there at the SPLA camp but my brother told me she would not be there till the marriage process was done. But she came every evening and took me to their house until my father returned from his mission. We spent the whole day talking about everything until evening. Time went by so fast I wasn't even paying attention my brother asked me if I knew who was coming. I said, "My father?"

He said, "No, just wait."

It was our stepmother. I had no idea what she looked like since I'd never seen her before. When she arrived, she shook my brother's hand. "This must be your brother, Chol?" she asked.

"Yes," my brother answered.

She lifted me up and while she was holding me said with a smile on her face. "I'm your mother, Agak Arop." After she told me her name, it rang the bell because my brother already told me her name. The only thing I was missing was how she looked. I couldn't imagine a happier moment. I felt like my mother was back to life. I was just looking at her and at my brother. He was smiling, looking at me. Then she put me down.

"I'm going to take you home. I don't want you to stay here. You are going to be home with me till your father comes back," she said.

So we went home with her and stayed at her house for a while. After my father came back from his mission, they had an agreement. During the daytime, we could go and spend the day with my father. In the evening, she came and took us home. This continued for a while till my father completed the marriage. According to Dinka tribe culture, her family had prepared her before she joined the new family.

New family- 16

In 1985, we moved to a village called Neel. It was a safer place than the SPLA camp. My father took us to Neel and stayed at one of my relative's house. It had been abandoned for a while so we settled there. Months later, my uncle Kiir brought cows to us and while we were there, he got married to his wife, Aluel Malith. She was very nice to us and we became one big family. I was the youngest kid in the family so I was so special for them. That was a great moment that felt like a family reunion. They gave my father a break not to worry about our being alone at the house because he was always at the SPLA camp. He could get an order anytime to go to the frontline.

Everything went back to the normal. On top of that, my stepmother was amazing. We spent almost two years in Neel, till the winter of 1986 when my father asked my uncle to take both families to the cattle camp to avoid that area because it was close to northern Sudan border and it was in winter time that the militants started their movement towards southern Sudan with their cows looking for grasslands. That made it one of the most dangerous seasons for residents who were bordered by Arab tribes to start cattle movement to Southern Sudan. The Arabs attacked by burning all houses down and chasing the residents away from their homes, moving them to the next village. Sometimes, they let their cows eat in the residents' fields, destroying all crops. When the owners resisted, the result was always negative way often just killing the owner. From past actions, people learned a lot. They knew that during the winter, they had to leave their homes and move far a way to avoid contact with militants. As a result, the residents at the border were always faced with attacks during the militants' movement.

That winter, my uncle took us to the Twic region. We passed through many villages and it took us about a month because on our way, every time when we entered a different village, people were kind and they asked us to rest at their homes for few days.

At the beginning of autumn, we moved back to Neel for the cultivation season. We stayed there and my father kept traveling back and forth. Sometimes, he stayed for a while. Before the end the autumn, he stopped coming home for a while. We had no news about him so my stepmother sent my uncle to the SPLM headquarters to see what happened. He got no answer; he was just told that he was okay and that he would return soon, but they couldn't tell where he was. We waited until the beginning of winter when my father sent someone asking the whole family to come where he was. The person told us to go to the Nuer region. I can't not recall name of the place. We started walking in a group. My uncle was with his wife and his family and in laws. No one spoke the Nuer language but my brother. We walked during the day and in the evening. We got to the nearest house and my brother asked them if we could stay in their yard for one night until we arrived where we were supposed to meet my father.

The good thing was that my father had a plan and none of us was aware of. In the morning, he called a family meeting and told us he had sold three cows for us to go into Northern Sudan. One for Kiir, one for his family and in laws and one for Dau and Chol, but the baby and his mother were not going. A few days later, we woke up early, even before the sun rose. He accompanied us for an hour and then he returned to the cattle camp where he was staying.

That was last time I saw my father. It was a very sad moment but there was no choice. He convinced us that he did not want our lives to be in danger. We started walking toward Mayom, at that time the only way to northern Sudan. Abyei road was closed as it was dangerous. Militants used to attack people going that way. So, we started our journey to Mayom. I can't recall how many days we walked, but it was far. We started walking in the morning and took our rest when the sun was up and it got too hot. We used to find a tree to rest under until evening and then started moving again. Always before it turned dark, we stopped at the closest house and asked them if they would let us stay in the yard to sleep only for a night.

We arrived at Mayom early in morning. My uncle said we had to find a temporary place and he would go first and check how much it would cost per person to rent a truck to go the rest of the way. We discovered many abandoned houses so we went to one of those and stayed.

The first day, we didn't have a luck. There were no trucks leaving. We waited and finally after days, one was ready to go Khartoum. Our final destination was the Omdurman public market. It was far but for us coming from the village, it was nothing. We started walking to Aalghemair, which is the part of the Omdurman district where a majority of our relatives resided. We reached there around evening time. You could imagine how tired we were, and we went to sleep immediately. Early in a morning, the first person I saw was Akoul Makol. She used to be our neighbor in Biemnom. I could see how sad she was about the whole situation. She asked my uncle if she could take us to her house so we went there. She gave us many clothes to change into and we spent the whole day there before she took us back to my uncle. For the first time, I met a majority of people from Biemnom including some of my childhood friends. We settled there for a while but not too long. Next we moved to Al Thawra with my uncle's family in-laws.

There, everything became totally strange. Every person I knew was also uncomfortable with the situation, but for my uncle it was great going to Aal ghemair. Every morning, he stayed with his age group and came back to us at night. Every day, he was seeing the people who knew us back in Biemnom. One day, my brother asked him if he could go with him to meet his childhood friends. He did and according to my brother, a friend of his suggested him to stay there with him and he would help him to find a job. The majority of the people worked at wealthy Arabs' houses as housekeepers. A week later, he returned to Al thawra very excited because his friend found him a job. He came to spend Sunday with me, but he had to go back Monday morning. He promised me that the next week he was going to take me with him if he found a job. Later, he returned with good news. The lady he worked for, had a sister who needed a kid to work for her; it was great news for me.

We went. I was so ready, even though I wasn't qualified to work yet, as I was just about ten years old. She employed me nonetheless, since she was just looking for a kid to send to a shop and wash dishes with a monthly salary of forty Sudanese pounds. One pound every Sunday because it was my only day off. I had no idea about the job. My brother convinced me that the important thing was that I had a place to eat, take a shower and wash clothes. Also this was the only way to keep me close to him. Otherwise, I had to go back to my uncle. So I took the job and it was very easy. I finished every day before eleven o'clock and then went to my brother till three o'clock during the dinner to get ready to wash dinner dishes. Everything went well so my brother decided we had to go to school because we had the whole evening free. Sometimes, we just went and played football (soccer). We enrolled. They put him in fourth grade but they put me in first grade based on my placement test. Still, I kept my job. We went to work in the morning and go to school in the evening. Class started at six o'clock and we continue till 1989. When my auntie Nyanapur Monyluak (my dad's cousin) came from South Sudan, she asked us to come and stay with her. She stopped me from working, as I was too young. She said I only needed to worry about school since she was going to provide me with all my school needs. I spent only a year with her and then I went to Wad- Madani.

In 1990, my clan, Manteing, spread the word all over north Sudan to all young men ranging from the age of eleven and above, to come to Wad-Madani to meet with the father of the generation. According to our culture, each generation had a person who was responsible and would name the generation. I did not count myself among those who had moved from childhood to manhood at that time so, my brother went to Wad-Madani. I stayed at school. I felt I had already seen guys from other clans who never made it back to school.

A month later, my brother returned and asked me to join this generation. I told him I already made my decision. I wanted to keep going to my school. He convinced me at least to go and attend the celebration. We went to Wad-Madani and when we arrived, everything was different. It was amazing, I had never seen anything like that in my whole life. Those who were scarred on their faces - the sign of moving to maturity - were respected and were totally different. When I met everyone, the only question was, "Are you ready?" If you said "no," ladies wouldn't shake your hand or talk to you. They didn't even tell their names. All they said were "We don't talk to little boys."

It didn't take me long to change my mind because there was nothing else where we were. People talked about how many days left and who would be the first and who would be the last person. A few days before the scarring took place, my uncle and his wife came from Khartoum to attend the occasion. According to our tradition, it had been decided from a long time ago whose family should go first, second and last. These were the main positions: Our position range was the second position. The first person was Kiir Boung, the second was Dau makuach (my older brother), followed by younger ones. I was the fifth person, then followed by everyone else. We were twenty-seven. Before the last was Chol monyaguek Kur yol and the last person was Bol Jongchol Kat.

1. Kiir Boung was representing Dhien Mayal Giir
2. Dau Makuach was representing Dhien Dau Godjok
3. Chol Monyaguek Kur yol representing Pannyankiir Kon Arieu
4. Bol Jongchol Kat was representing Dhien Kon Arieu

We spent seven days indoors with no contact with other people except cousins from other generations who were ahead of us. Ladies brought food and gave it to the guys. After seven days, our elders came and began to name us with names from bull's colors. Those colors had been divided according to how many sons there were within the family. There were particular colors given for the first-born son, second, third, fourth and so on. In addition, they explained to us all the relationship and division of Mantieng sub-clans and Pajuac (Pagiir) itself. I also learned about how many relatives divisions there were in Mantieng.

1. Pakuei
2. Dhien de yor
3. Dhien de Achiek
4. Dhien de Chan
5. Dhien de Kueth
6. Pajuac (pagiir)
7. Dhien Dieng

Pajauc (Pagiir) itself is divided to the following

1. Dhien Mayal Giir
2. Dhien Kon Arieu
3. Dhien Chol Baak (Dhien Kueth who lately became independent)
4. Pannyankiir kon Arieu (originally from Patier Mijuan and they migrated to Pajuac and settled with Dhien Kon Arieu where their grandmother Nyankiir was originally from.
5. Dhien Dau Godjok.

Dhien Dau Godjok is divided into three subdivisions.

1. Pan de Godjok Dau
2. Pan de Koshkon Dau
3. Pan de Majak Dau

Pan de Godjok Dau migrated to Dhien Kiir Arop in Mijuan clan where their grandmother Atinet Arop Kiir was from, Pan de koshkon and Pan Majak remained in Mantieng clan.

After many lessons, they allowed us to talk to people outside. Also, those who knew how to write songs started coming for songs. Songs were all about how brave you are and how you were not embarrassed. No matter what the situation was, you would never leave your family behind. All songs went to my brother. I was a second son in a family, and according to our culture, the second son had less priority.

The only song was me was "ku col mangnog, rur mangnog wach luou da acien piou aliir." This in English languages meant, "Even Chol blue fox, (blue was a bull's color given to me by my uncle) doesn't have a fear in his heart."

After thirty days, we were dismissed. The majority of us came from different cities, so everyone returned. Unfortunately, I ended up with no plan of going back to Khartoum or going back to school. Everything totally changed, including the job I had been doing. I felt the job was an embarrassment for a man. The only job was available that I could feel more comfortable with was a construction job but it was not easy for me because of my age. I tried many times to get a job but people refused to hire me, telling me I was too young for the job.

Everything fell apart. The good thing was that I did not have to worry about what to eat or where to live. At that time one of my uncle's wives, Agoon Monyroor Maker, took a huge responsibility for those who were there without parents including those who were unwilling to return. It was one of the greatest moments I had. No job and no school, just freedom for almost for three years, enjoying the manhood life.

In 1992, my mind started to reset to manhood and traditional things. I went to my auntie and asked her help finding me a housekeeping job. She was serious and said many times she had been telling me about the housekeeping jobs and I kept saying this job is embarrassing for a young man like me. But more embarrassing was when you walked around without a job. People would consider that you a lazy person.

A few days later, she came and told me about a job I was completely uncomfortable with. Every day, before I went to work, I waited until the street was cleared to make sure no one would see me entering the Arab house. After a few months, I realized that I was not the only one who was doing that kind of job. It made me more comfortable and I started to like my job. I became very close to the people I was working for, especially one of their sons who was about my age. We become best friends and I started to teach him few words in Dinka and he taught me a few words in English.

That inspired me and gave me a motivation about going back to school. When I went to register, my friend Omar gave me two pencils and congratulated for going back to school. That time, he was in the last year of his secondary school. After he finished, he went to Khartoum University to study with his older brother and sister. He had to leave Wad-Madani. His family had another house in Khartoum but no one lived there. His family decided that instead having all three of them going to stay at boarding school; they could stay at the house and take me with them to keep the housekeeping work and laundry for them.

We went to Khartoum according to the plan. The good thing was that I was familiar with Khartoum area. Few days later, I started looking for an evening school so I could continue with my school. Before we moved to Khartoum, I finished book one. I was ready for book two, which was considered second grade.

I went to Omdurman looking for an evening school that taught English. All schools around in that area taught only Arabic. Luckily, I was directed to an evangelical church that offered basic English classes from book one to book six. On the day I went to register, they told me there were only a few days left in the school year and book two had about seven lessons left. They told me I could join the class and I didn't have to take the final exams because I was going to start with new people who were starting book two a week after the final examinations.

It was not my intention because I finished book one and bought book two. The whole time, I had been reading at home I had covered the most part of the book. So a day before exams, I asked my teacher if I could take the final examination with the class. He told me yes. If I was lucky and passed the exam, I could proceed to book three. That way I didn't have to spend six months in book- two. I took the exam and it was easier than what I expected.

It took a week for the teacher to make arrangements for a new class. After that, we went back to school before he announced the result. He asked me to stand up and asked me how long I had been in this class. I told him just a week. He congratulated me! He said I was going to book- three. Then he asked the class to clap their hands for me. I was so proud of myself. That encouraged me more to continue my schooling. However, the more you progress, the higher the fees. The class fee was based on the number of subjects you were taking. I came up with a decision that since school kept getting more expensive, I could stop at primary six because I could not afford to pay the primary seven fee and the system for primary seven was different too. All students had to pay the fee for the whole school year at one time and there was no way I could come up with that much money. Still, I continued with my housekeeping job. They gave me a room where I could sleep and study at night. During that time, I travelled to Wad-Madani with them to the main house where their relatives were because their parents were in Kuwait. Their parents only came to spend vacations with them in Khartoum. Every time, they brought me bags of clothes and shoes. I never worried about buying clothes or shoes since they were kind to me, especially Omer, their son who was about my age; he was just like a brother to me.

During my school time in 1995, I had met a guy named Mathiang Bol Ajing. He was from Twic Gogrial. This guy was amazing and became my best friend. He was not just not a best friend; he was my brother and the only person I trusted. He was always there for me, and the closest person to me. We lived in the same area called Omdurman. Sometimes, when I didn't have money for transportation to go school, he would tell me it was okay since he was there for me. I remember his words of encouragement. He always used to say we have to push this life very slowly.

In 1997, I finished the primary six. I was supposed to register for primary seven but I didn't have enough money to pay the school fee. I was at the point to just stop according to my plan. One day, Dr. El fadiel was about to go back to Kuwait after his vacation, but he had to go to Wad-Madani first to say goodbye to his mother and to the rest of his relatives. I went with him and his family to Wad-Madani for few days and returned to Khartoum. A day before Dr. El fadiel left for Kuwait, I was cleaning the balcony when something caught my eye. I saw him sitting in a yard inside the house and some of the neighbors were shaking his hands to say good bye to him. He gave each one a stack of money. I stopped what I was doing and watched them closely to make sure what I was seeing was real. Then I went inside to ask his wife what he was doing. She said that every year, El fadiel has a special badge for poor people. It didn't take me long after I got that answer. "What about me?" I asked her. "I'm poor too."

She laughed it off, so I returned to finish what I was doing. I remembered that day it was Friday, and all his kids were home. A few minutes later, I heard him yelling, "Chol! Chol!" Before I reached his room, I saw everyone looking at me in fear. They thought I had done something wrong. When I entered his room, he asked me to close the door. He said that in the house, there was no difference between me and his son Omer, that what I said earlier to Fatahia was wrong.

That moment I was ready with my answer. I told him I was about to drop out from school because it was getting to expensive and I could not afford to pay that much. I would needs about seven hundred Sudanese ponds plus school uniforms and books. Then he asked me what else? I said that was all. He said that from that day onward, he was going to start paying for my school and special payments for books and school uniforms. If he was not around, his son,Mohammed, would help me with everything. In addition to that, his son was going to buy me a bicycle. That way I wouldn't have to worry about transportation. This would continue until I get my Sudan certificate, which was considered as a high school diploma.

My American dream- 18

In 2000, after I had married my wife, I was in my final year of secondary school. I had one more year to get my Sudan certificate. Getting married was probably one of the biggest mistakes I had made, since it was totally a different lifestyle that before. With the help of my friends, I found a house with only one room. I made another room for my stepmother. Unfortunately, the same year, something happened about my job. I was not making enough to support the family, which put me back into a life of struggle.

One night, I had a dream. In my sleep, my brother, Dau, came with a stack of money in his hand. He said to take the money to repay the people I owed. When I woke up in the morning, I started to tell my wife and step mother about the dream. They were laughing at me and my stepmother said maybe because I was broke, I dreamt about money. A few minutes after we finished drinking tea, my cousin came in saying he had a message from my brother, that my brother was in America and wanted to talk to me the next day at ten o'clock at Thon Mongrage. He said I had a phone appointment and my brother was going to call me. Once he finished talking, I turned to my stepmother and told her that my dream was true. I had not talked to my brother in six years.

"How did you get married and what about school?" he asked when we spoke. "How are you supporting the family? You must be in too much trouble." "Yes, I'm in the middle of debts," I told him, "I owe many people money." "I'm going to send you enough money to clear yourself out and don't give up on your school," he said. "Come back tomorrow for another phone appointment." He told me the place where I could receive the money when I returned. He gave me the address of place and the amount was eight hundred US dollars. I had no idea what the value of the US dollar was compared to the Sudanese pound but, the person called Dau Nyuar kiir, whom I used to get the phone calls appointment, worked at the bank The money was sent to his name, so he knew exactly how much that amount was worth in Sudanese pounds. He told me to get a taxi and when I got home, put it in a safe place. He gave me the money and I did exactly what he told me. The next day, I started paying everybody I owed and things went back to normal.

In 2002, I finished my secondary school, thus completing my plan, but the situation was still bad, so I decided to leave the country, looking to start a new life. We began the process. A few weeks before I left Sudan I had a son and had to stop the process and add him on my passport.

Finally, I left for Egypt in January, 2003. I didn't have a plan to stay. I just took a risk. The bus driver took us to the church where many Sudanese gathered every Monday morning to check if there were new people who had come to Egypt. Luckily, one of my longtime friends, Atem Manyiel Yut, showed up. I always called him cousin as his auntie was married to my uncle. He was surprised to see me. He took me to his house at Dar El malik. The next day, the two guys from Biemnom, monyluak Ngor Malek Abiel and Kon Toruk Monywach came to my cousin's house. I had known them we were in Biemnom. They were childhood friends and we used to called ourselves "Biemnom children." I hadn't seen them in many years and it was amazing to see them again. We spent the whole day just talking. Before they left, they told my cousins and me the reason for their visit. They were there to take me and my family to Ain shames. That place had more people from Biemnom, but I convinced them they were my friends and Atem was my cousin. Since I was already settled in his house, I would stay. The only thing I needed them to do was to help me find my own apartment in Ain shames. That way I would be closer to them. They left and asked my cousin to bring me anytime to Ain shames. During that time in Cairo, people were living in groups. If you were looking for a person from Biemnom, Ain Shames was the only place where you could find them.

My first visit to Ain Shames was to a few homes to visit families. Then we went to a coffee shop where the guys spent the evening. I was surprised to see everyone and some I had not seen in a long time, some of them for many years. One childhood friend, Chan Achuiel, volunteered to help me to find an apartment. Finally, we found one but the plan was to find a bigger apartment to move both our families.

My volunteering Job in Egypt- 19

After I moved in to the new place, I was taken to the United Nations office for refugees and immigration to report myself. To get a legal permit in Egypt and to avoid deportation, I was given an appointment to come back with my information. I was not aware that some people charged for completing the application. I asked my friend to bring copy of his application to see what it looked like. When I looked at it, it was not hard for me to do it myself I prepared it and then I returned for an interview. I passed it and was given another appointment for resettlement. While I was waiting, one of my best friends, Matat Akol, followed by Angelo Bol, teamed up on doing the application process. They knew how to read and write Arabic more but I knew English more.

We came up with an idea instead of going to look for someone to complete an application, I had changed my mind. I told them it was not a good idea. People were acting very strange. Sometimes, when they got rejected they blamed it on the person who completed the application for them. But my friend Chan Achuiel told me to remember that no matter what, you cannot stop people from talking and there are people who are really in need. We came to an agreement that we were going to do it voluntarily with no charge.

The applicant has to be responsible for two things when going for an interview, money for typing and money for the transportation. The office was ready but nobody wanted to take the risk. One day, my friend Matat Akol Chol who happened to be a member of the office went for resettlement.

Things didn't go well. He was given a letter for local resettlement in Cairo, so we went to the coffee shop as usual. I joked that if he went and got a form for the Australia embassy I could practice on his form. Somehow, he took it seriously and next day early in a morning, he showed up at my apartment and said if I didn't practice on his, whose form I'm going to practice on? In addition to that, I didn't have money to pay the guy. He said I should just do it, so I started working on his application.

It took me almost four days to finish the application. I gave it to him to take it to Australian embassy and only one week later the embassy called him. He came to me and said he got a phone call from the embassy and they wanted him and his family to go there tomorrow with an interpreter. We had to be there by 8:00 am but, no details yet. That was really scary. We were waiting uncomfortably for the morning to come. I went with him as his interpreter. Minutes later, they called him and asked where his translator was. I was right beside him. I said I was the translator and we went inside the office. The interview lasted for only twenty minutes. After that, he handed me papers for the medical exam and asked me to explain them to him. A medical exam is another step for qualification. All family members had to pass or the application would be denied. Then he thanked me for coming. He walked with me to the elevator and I cannot explain how happy we were. We spent the rest of the day very happy; we can't wait for evening to come. We went to the coffee shop and after that, he did something very amazing. He went to the waiter and told him to ask all Sudanese who were around what they wanted to drink. Then he announced to congratulate him as he was going to Australia soon. He went to an interview this morning and everything went successfully. He really appreciated me for volunteering my time to complete his application and going with him that morning as his translator.

A few minutes later, few people started asking me what I did with the application. I was just very polite. I said I did it voluntarily for the Biemnom Association because people had had their files closed. Some had been rejected and were pending appeal now. Australia was the only option for them.

The next day, I went to the coffee shop as usual and sat. Even before I requested my tea, the waiter brought my favorite tea. I was trying to pay but he said it had already been paid. After I finished, two gentlemen pulled their chairs beside me and they introduced themselves to me. One of them said they have been waiting there almost three hours. He needed my help about his closed file. He did an application and had been denied. He had no hope for anything except this form for Australia and he didn't have money for the guy to complete it. He heard that I didn't charge as this was like a voluntary society to help people from Biemnom. In Cairo, our society is not the only people who need helps. The fact that I do it voluntarily is a blessing," he said, "Help people and anything good you do to people, God will reward you one day."

I took their forms and said I would call them when they were ready. After I finished, I called them few days later. Everything changed. Every time, I went to the coffee shop, I found people waiting for me with applications. Those who were close came straight to my apartment where I lived and there was no way to tell them not to come. I remember one day, I woke up and before I even washed my face, I had about six people waiting in the living room. I was not taking it seriously, but looking at the way people were acting, the team and I came up with a rule. Anyone who had an application needed their case to be translated into English, written or oral translation, had to call first or come to the coffee shop to make an appointment. After that, they could come to my house. It was the most amazing thing I had ever done in my life. People didn't even call me by name; they only called me "Sir."

One day, a person called my home phone and my wife answered it. It was around one o'clock in the afternoon but in Egypt, people used to stay up all night and sleep all day. The person said he needed to talk to me. Was I was sleeping? I was right beside the phone and my wife covered the phone. She handed it to me in a very funny way and said, "Here you go, Mr. Chol, someone needs to speak to you."

I just smiled and said to her, "Get used to it."

During my volunteer work, I learned many things about people - which people are patient, which are aggressive and which people are polite. Some don't care about other people's feeling.

Others never try to hurt other people's feeling. One of the greatest people I met was Chol Kur Monydeeng. This man came to Egypt when the United Nations was not resettling people. The only way was the Australia Embassy but, it was very important for people go to the United Nations office to get a refugee card to be a legal resident in Egypt first because the Egyptians could deport them back to Sudan at any time.

He came to me through our conversation; he touched my heart in a very different way. He respected me the first day I met him. He introduced himself to me and explained how we were related. His grandmother, Piot Kon, was from my sub-clan. He asked me if I could fill his application so I asked him to bring some information like his passport and kid's birth certificate. He brought them to me and put them somewhere in my papers.

I was not feeling any pressure from him. I was doing those who were very aggressive first. Every time he met me he was very polite and the only thing he said was, "Did you get chance to look at my application?"

My answer to him was always, "I'm busy."

That has been going on almost for three weeks. No one can wait that long. One day he asked me if his application was ready. I said yes, it was in the library. We need to go and make corrections and check misspellings before printing it. He just kept asking, "When can I come and get it?"

I told him, "Tomorrow morning."

The next day, early in the morning, my roommate, Chan Achuiel's wife, heard a knock at the door. Her room was close to the main door so she went and opened the door. She came back and knocked at my room. I opened the door and was told someone was waiting for me in the living room. It was eight in a morning, I was really upset. I went to the living room and even before I said something, he said, "Grandfather's son, I'm so sorry to wake you up. I didn't know what time you wanted me to come and I didn't want to be late for you,"

I was confused about what to say but, I calmed myself down. "Go to the library and wait for me there. I'm going to wash my face and will be there in a few minutes," I told him.

On my way to the library, I found forty Egyptian pounds. I looked around, holding the money. I thought maybe somebody was going to claim it but, no one was there. I went to the library and asked him if he dropped any money. He said no. I thought this must be a reward for me for waking up early in a morning.

On my translations, I went through many things, funny, sad, and misunderstandings. One day, a young man came to me and asked me to be his interrupter for an interview. I wrote down his interview information and a week later I went to the Australian embassy. While we were in a lobby waiting to be called, he told me he didn't want to lie. He wanted to tell the truth to the officer who was going to interview him. I asked him what he meant. He said some words in this case are not true. I told him we have to go by the case, if we change anything, the officer would think the case was not true and he could be rejected.

He answered that God's kingdom was not in USA or Canada or Australia. I thought he was not serious about it. His name was called and we went inside the office. The lady started asking questions and he kept answering questions out of the application. I was familiar with his case. I translated it from Arabic to English before he applied, so I tried to make corrections but, he started an argument with me and said he already told me to tell her exactly the truth during our discussion.

The lady realized something was not right. She asked me if everything was all right. He answered no. Then the lady put all papers together and asked me if I could explain what was going on. The young man was still saying to me, "You must tell her the truth."

At that moment I didn't have anything to say besides explaining our earlier discussion. I told the lady everything and after I finished talking, she thanked me for coming and said she would send him a letter about the decision on his case, which was a very clear disqualification.

On our way to the bus station, he kept thanking God for listening to him. I told him if he didn't want to go to Australia, he shouldn't have come for an interview. He said there was no way I could confess if he didn't come. I was shocked and asked him why brought me all the way to witness his confession. That was one of the funniest thing I had seen during my translation days.

I took another young man for an interview. Everything went well and after the interview finished, the officer began to explain to him that his application had been accepted. The next step was medical examinations. Before she finished explaining, the young man broke down and started crying. The officer and I were surprised. The lady asked me if he was okay, so I asked him if he was okay. After he stopped crying, he said the interview reminded him about the whole situation he had been through and apologized to the lady.

On our way home, he shook my hand and thanked me for coming with a "sorry." He hadn't meant to put me in his sad situation but, now he was happy and that was the one of the saddest situations.

Sometimes, I found myself in a middle of disappointment, since I had been in Cairo and used to live in Ain shames. Cairo is a big city and some areas across Ain shames take time to reach. One day, a lady came from El maadi with a direction where she can found me. After she arrived at the coffee shop, she stood far away and started yelling. There were many people and one of my friends named Achuiel Chol recognized her. He went to see what she needed. After a short conversation, e returned and said she was my guest. I stood up and walked towards her before we reached her; she started asking Achueil where the interrupter was. She asked if I was not around. She was told this is the only place where he could be. I found my friend ashamed and did not know what to say. That was a nonstop question till we approached her and introduced myself to her by name. I was really disappointed that she would think I was not there. The two of us were coming towards her. I made an appointment to come to her house which, I didn't normally do, but I did considering her distance.

She was uncomfortable. I could tell from the conversation we had. I took her phone number. That way when I get to the bus stop, I could call for someone to come and walk us to her home. The next day, my friend John Arop Mangar and I went to her house and took all her information. After that, I started to give her some ideas about how I do my translation work. After I finished talking, she said she was sorry for her attitude when she was looking for me. According to our society, people always treat you by the way you dress and that day she saw me I didn't dress like the person she was looking for. I took her form and a week later, I brought it back to her. When she was scheduled for an interview, I went with her for the translation. Everything went well and the day before she left for Australia, she invited me and all friends to her farewell party. It was great thing as she introduced me as a special guest for the party. That changed me from being disappointed with her to motivate me to help more people.

That time, I was waiting my cases to be accepted by the United Nations, but I didn't know where I was supposed to go. I was given a slip with a resettlement date. It was almost a year of waiting and finally, the date came. We went there for another interview and before the decision, everything went well. The lady chose United States to be my new home. That was the first step. The second step was screening. The final step was an interview with department of the homeland security. I was called for the interview and medical examinations. Then I was scheduled for a flight, followed by orientation to tell me a little bit about how is in the United States. That was the most interesting part of the process because I was leaving for America. That was the first time I got to taste MacDonald's food. The lady explained to us as a very easy and recommended food and said they were open 24 hours.

On June 3rd, 2005, before I left for America, the Biemnom Association organized a very nice farewell party. Mario Mongkuer, the general secretary, put flyers all over the main places where Sudanese had SPLA chapters, coffee shops and churches. It was great to see a huge crowd coming for me to say good bye. The sad part was, the next day when all my close friends and relatives accompanied me to the airport. I was sad about leaving them, but at the same time, I was happy because I was just few hours away from my American dream. That night, we took a flight from Egypt to Germany, to New York to Washington DC and I arrived at my final destination in Roanoke Virginia on June 7th, 2005.

As soon as a I approached the lobby, the first person I saw was my brother Dau makuach and his friend. After nine years of separation, I met him again. My brother and his friend took my family and me to the refugee and immigrations office to report in and finish the process.

On my arrival to Roanoke, the refugee and immigrations office did not expect me to come to Roanoke. I was supposed to go to Salt Lake City, Utah but, my brother and his friend changed my address four days before departure to America so, there was no place for me and my family to live. I had to stay with my brother and his friend until my apartment was ready to move in. It didn't take long to be ready, and then I moved in at Valley View village. The situation was different from what I was thinking. There were about ten apartments rented by Sudanese that made it easy for me not to worry about transportation till I bought my first car.

Printed in the United States
By Bookmasters